HAPPY

HAPPY

50 MINDFULNESS AND RELAXATION EXERCISES

TO BOOST YOUR MOOD

EVERY DAY

Dr. Arlene Unger
and Lona Eversden

METRO BOOKS
New York

METRO BOOKS
New York

An Imprint of Sterling Publishing Co., Inc.
1166 Avenue of the Americas
New York, NY 10036

This book is not intended as a substitute for medical or
psychotherapeutic advice, and readers are advised to consult a healthcare
professional for individual concerns and to check that the exercises are
suitable for their particular needs. The creators of the work and the
publisher cannot be held liable for any actions that may be taken as
a consequence of the information in this book.

ISBN 978-1-4351-6445-1

For information about custom editions, special sales,
and premium and corporate purchases, please contact Sterling
Special Sales at 800-805-5489 or specialsales@sterlingpublishing.com.

Manufactured in China by Toppan Leefung Printers Limited

2 4 6 8 10 9 7 5 3 1

www.sterlingpublishing.com

Credits:
Publisher: Kerry Enzor
Co-author: Lona Eversden
Project Editor: Anna Southgate
Designer: Dave Jones
Senior Editor: Philippa Wilkinson
Production Manager: Zarni Win

CONTENTS

INTRODUCTION

We all want to feel content and we spend a large part of our lives in the pursuit of happiness. We look for work that fulfills us, partners who cherish us, families that support and nurture us, and friends that make us laugh. Or do we? Perhaps surprisingly, our lifestyles and our actions often suggest that we do not strive for happiness above all else, but instead sacrifice feeling happy for other goals, such as making money, gaining social status, and avoiding negatives, such as discomfort or boredom.

Today, in the developed world at least, there is more potential for individual happiness than ever before. We have more freedom, more money, and greater opportunities than our predecessors could have dreamed of. So, in theory, we should be happier than ever before. But for many of us, it doesn't feel like that. People consistently report having little time for leisure, not enough money to do what they really want, and—even when money is not an issue—that material wealth does not lead to true happiness. The fact is that modern living is stressful. We are increasingly connected by technology and disconnected from nature; our friendships are becoming more widespread and more superficial as we chat online but not in person; and our workplaces are increasingly controlled by multinational corporations, making it more difficult for us to see the direct results of our labor in the way that our ancestors did. This has all led to a general decline in our mental health, with more than three-quarters of visits to the physician estimated to be stress-related.

Happiness 1, 2, 3

So what do we need to be happy? There's no precise recipe, of course, because we are all different and motivated by different things, but some psychologists define a happy life as one that includes:

1. **Pleasure**: Doing things for sheer enjoyment.

2. **Meaning**: Feeling that our lives are worthwhile, and that we make a difference.

3. **Engagement**: Being connected to friends, family, and our communities.

Taking control of your happiness

We cannot control all of our life circumstances, but psychologists believe that making small changes to our daily lives, outlook, and attitude can have a significant effect on our emotional well-being. It has been estimated that half our happiness is determined by genetic factors, 10 percent by our life circumstances, and 40 percent by our daily activities and other factors under our control.

This book is all about that 40 percent. It will help you redress the happiness balance in your life through 50 inspiring exercises and visualizations. You can dip in and out of it, doing whichever exercises catch your eye, or you can work your way through it, chapter by chapter. Some exercises are instant fixes, others will kickstart a whole new way of living. They draw on well-attested studies and therapies, including cognitive behavioral therapy (CBT), emotional brain training (EBT), mindfulness-based stress reduction (MBSR), affirmations, and visualizations.

My happy score

Take a few moments to look at the 1, 2, 3 list and evaluate your life out of 10 on each point.

Pleasure .../10

Meaning .../10

Engagement .../10

If one of your scores is significantly lower than the others, this gives you some idea as to where you can most effectively focus your energies if you want to boost your overall happiness.

TEN **HAPPY HABITS** TO **ADOPT**

Happy people appreciate the present moment rather than spending all their time in the past or future. Here are ten ways to be happier:

1 **Surround yourself** with other happy people.

2 **Prioritize activities** that make you feel good.

3 **Take responsibility** for your own happiness and don't blame others when things go wrong.

4 **Get enough** sleep, eat well, and exercise regularly.

5 **Forgive yourself** when you slip up.

6 **Take pleasure** in the small things.

7 **Don't compare** yourself to other people, but welcome the success of others.

8 **Get out** into nature regularly.

9 **Be resilient** when setbacks occur.

10 **Give to others** through kindness, compliments, and donations.

When to seek help
We can regulate our moods and boost our well-being through self-help measures, such as the ones in this book. But if your emotional issues are continual or they impact on your everyday life, relationships, or work, you should consult your physician or a professional therapist for individual advice and support.

Emotional brain training

This therapy, sometimes abbreviated to EBT, is based on the idea that stress becomes encoded in the brain and, over time, can take over as our default way of being. It offers a variety of tools that can be used to identify and rewire stress circuits, replacing them with more joyful ways of thinking. Emotional brain training aims to stimulate the brain's reward centers in positive ways and, with regular practice, this can change the brain's default stress setting to one geared toward awareness and joy. There is also a focus on a healthy lifestyle to promote vitality.

Cognitive behavioral therapy

Cognitive behavioral therapy, or CBT, is used to treat depression and anxiety, and like emotional brain training, is very much focused on dealing with issues in the here and now rather than delving into the past. It is based on the idea that we can change the way we feel and act by training ourselves to think in more positive ways. This is done by identifying and challenging negative beliefs, and by replacing them with more positive and constructive ways of thinking. Cognitive behavioral therapy also includes specific stress-reduction techniques and focuses on the benefits of exercise, healthy eating, and good sleep.

Mindfulness-based stress reduction

This therapy—MBSR for short—teaches us to focus on the present reality without getting distracted by self-criticism, or by thoughts of past or future events. This "being in the moment" is a powerful therapeutic technique that has been proven to increase feelings of happiness over time. Both mindfulness and meditation are used to encourage us to notice what is going on in our minds and bodies. This helps us to recognize signs of stress or anxiety so we can better deal with them. It also helps us to become less reactive in our actions.

Visualizations and affirmations

Many of the exercises in this book comprise or include an element of visualization or affirmation. Scientists have found that we can react in the same way to an imaginary situation as we can to a real-life one. In one experiment, they discovered that visualizing ourselves exercising can actually build muscle tone. You can also use visualization to boost your mood or aid relaxation. Similarly, affirmations are a way of reinforcing positive thinking habits through repeating short positive messages. They are used in cognitive behavioral therapy, and several feature within the chapters of this book.

Below: Life is always a balancing act, but the exercises in this book will help you to find moments of happiness in every day.

RISE
AND SHINE

Are you an owl or a lark? Studies have found that people who identified themselves as morning people or "larks" tend to be much more positive about life than "night owls." They often take greater charge of their lives, use quiet uninterrupted time first thing for goal-setting and planning, and are better at anticipating and minimizing problems. One reason for this is that society is geared more toward daylight than darkness, leaving night owls out of sync with the world around them.

Whenever possible, set the happiness tone for your day with a morning-focused schedule. Get up early and see if you can make time for some form of outdoor exercise. Physical activity has a clear link with happiness levels, and exercising outside means you get longer exposure to sunlight, which is important for positive moods.

If you need to change your habits, begin by tweaking your schedule: Stick to regular bed- and waking-up times to reset your body clock and get up half an hour earlier each day. Then you can set about raising your happiness quotient with this chapter's mood-boosting exercises.

01 GREET THE SUN

As far back as the Stone Age, people worshipped sunlight. At nightfall they prayed for sunny days; by morning they would rejoice in the sun's healing powers. Today, thanks to medical research, we know that the sun is good for our immune system. It also triggers the neurotransmitters serotonin and oxytocin, which can elevate our mood. Cognitive behavioral therapy stresses the idea that our positive beliefs about the future can shape and influence our attitude. This exercise helps you benefit from sunlight upon awakening just as our ancient predecessors did.

1 As you are rubbing your eyes awake, take notice of the natural light pouring into your bedroom.

2 Instead of turning on artificial light, open the blinds, curtains, or shutters.

3 Stand in the sun's light and make an exaggerated welcoming gesture. Allow yourself simply to drink in the warmth, light, and positive energy of those glorious rays as you get ready to start your day.

WHEN TO DO IT

This is a good exercise to do at the start of your day. By training yourself to wake up to sunshine, you can expect to face each day in a better, happier mood.

02 FEEL THE LOVE

Wouldn't it be fabulous if we woke up to being acknowledged for all the wonderful things we do during our lifetime? Whether or not we feel we have earned it, all of us deserve to be applauded at the beginning of each day. According to emotional brain training our brain is reward-driven and our need for love and gratitude shouldn't be overlooked—it is perfectly reasonable to receive and accept praise from others. Try this visualization at the start of each day.

1 As you lie in bed, before fully waking, imagine your bedroom filled with close family members and friends. Just before you open your eyes, listen for their enthusiastic applause.

2 Now open your eyes and see their smiling faces. As you gently wipe any residue sleep from your eyes, stand before your loved ones with a bright, beaming smile and throw your arms out in a wide embrace.

3 Now you are ready to return their love. Before leaving your bedroom for the day, wave good-bye to your friends and family members and blow them a kiss.

WHEN TO DO IT

Try this visualization every morning for one month, until the applause you hear becomes second nature. See yourself awaken every day with more spontaneity and spring in your step.

TOP **FIVE** WAYS
to get up earlier

Place your alarm across the
room, so you have to get out
of bed to turn it off

Smile as soon as your alarm sounds

Tell yourself:
"I love getting up early
in the morning"

Keep a cozy robe next to the
bed so you can stay warm

Track your progress; tick your calendar
every time you get up early

03 THE MINDFUL SHOWER

However busy you may be, there are always oases of time in which you can experience the joy of the moment. Take a simple shower, for example. You may see this as something to get through as quickly as possible before getting on with your day. In mindfulness, however, we discover that a shower can offer a cascade of sensation with which to engage—and it can provide an opportunity to find peace in a busy morning.

1 Before you turn on the shower, take a moment to acknowledge that the next few minutes are all you are concerned with. Decide to give all your attention to the experience of showering, just as it is this morning.

2 As you step into the shower, notice how the water gushes over you like a natural waterfall. Allow yourself to experience the different sensations this creates on the skin: the warmth, the wetness, the soft pressure. Feel your wet hair on your head, and the touch of your hands as you wash yourself.

3 Turn your attention to sounds you can hear— the hiss of the water as it comes out of the showerhead, and the way in which it drums on the hard walls and floor. Be aware of any other sounds that occur—the squeak as you squeeze the shampoo bottle and the noise your fingers make as they rub lather into your hair.

4 Look around you and notice the patterns that the water and the condensation make on the walls, the color of the soap or shampoo.

WHEN TO DO IT

Every morning! This can be a great way to introduce a few meditative moments into your daily routine. If you live with other people, ask them not to interrupt you as you take these few minutes for yourself.

5 Allow yourself to experience the aromas of the shower, too—the fruity or herbal notes in the soap you use, the smell of your own skin.

6 From time to time, you'll notice that your attention has wandered. As soon as you are aware of this happening, gently bring your focus back to the sights, sounds, sensations, or aromas that are your experience in this moment.

7 When you finish the shower, turn off the water, noticing how that action feels. Step out carefully. Gently dry yourself with a soft towel, pausing to take note of how that feels and sounds, too.

8 Take a moment or two to breathe deeply before getting on with your morning routine.

GO COLD

A cold shower in the morning will get your body into full alert—the shock of the cold makes you breathe deeper and your heart race. This is your body's attempt to increase your oxygen intake and so keep warm. It gives you an instant energy boost that is great for your mood. There's also research to show that daily cold showers boost your immune system.

04 FLOWER GAZE

Being in the presence of flowers makes us feel happy, say researchers at Harvard University, and theirs is just one of several studies that confirm the positive effect of flowers on our mood. Here's how to give yourself a floral boost first thing.

1 Have cut flowers in your kitchen. Most people spend time here in the morning, and catching sight of a bunch of flowers will help you feel less anxious, more positive, and more compassionate. Since the kitchen is where people tend to gather, everyone will benefit in the same way.

2 If you have a garden, head out there and look at the flowers each morning before work. Or take your morning coffee at a window from which you can see your plants. If you don't have a garden, plant up a window box where you can see it.

3 Alternatively, close your eyes and spend a few minutes visualizing a glorious bouquet of flowers. Make the image as detailed as you can—include the feel of the petals and the flowers' aroma.

WHEN TO DO IT

Engage with the beauty of flowers each morning, to help set yourself up for a joyful day.

FLOWER CARE

To make the most of the flowers you buy for your home, cut the stems before placing in water and add a little plant food, so they last longer.

PERSONAL AFFIRMATION

I believe in myself

05   SAY IT, BELIEVE IT

Can you talk yourself into happiness? Cognitive behavioral therapy argues that you can, and that one of the ways to do so is through the use of affirmations. By consciously thinking self-affirming thoughts we can challenge unhelpful thinking habits. Over time this can help to change our attitude for the better, which in turn transforms the way we feel about ourselves. Try these tips to create your own affirmations.

1 Choose a negative thought that you habitually think about yourself—perhaps, "I am so lazy at making new friends" or "I am so dull."

2 Write a short positive statement that directly counters this—"I feel lazy when it comes to making new friends, but I just need to assert myself more." Make sure the statement is wholly positive, expressed in the present tense, and uses words that resonate with you.

3 Repeat your affirmation ten times in the morning and at intervals during the day. Take a breath before you say it and express yourself with conviction. You can also try singing or chanting your affirmation—some people find it easier to connect with it this way. Believe in yourself!

WHEN TO DO IT

Affirmations work best if done every day and repeated often. Try writing your positive affirmation on a card and keeping it in your wallet or purse. Every time you reach for your purse you will notice it and this will serve as a reminder to say your inspiring words.

06 STAND TALL

If you are feeling miserable, look at how you are standing or sitting. Unhappy people tend to adopt a slouched posture. Conversely, slouching can also trigger feelings of sadness—psychologists call this link "embodied cognition." Here's a quick way to use your body to shift your mindset.

1 Find a wall and stand with your heels, bottom, and shoulder blades touching it. Your lower back curves inward naturally, so should not make contact with the wall.

2 Lower your chin a little and keep your head slightly away from the wall. Imagine yourself standing tall like a giraffe.

3 Maintain this position for 20–30 seconds and then move away from the wall, keeping the posture. If possible, walk around for another minute or two before sitting down again.

WHEN TO DO IT

Do this before you leave your home in the morning. Try to maintain the posture as you leave the house and start your journey.

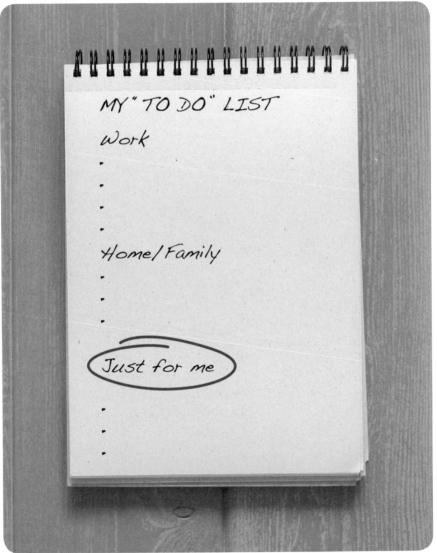

07 PLAN FOR POSITIVITY

Do you often wake up in the morning with a groan? Use the scheduling tool from cognitive behavioral therapy to make time for self-nurture and to give yourself something to look forward to. Looking after your own needs is key to increasing your happiness potential. The to-do list on the opposite page can serve as a template.

1 Set your alarm for 15 minutes earlier than you need to get up. That way, you make a little space in the morning for joy, rather than just rushing out the door. Sit and drink your coffee or tea in peace, meditate, or listen to music (see pages 58–61).

2 Set a morning routine. Follow the same pattern every day. The fewer decisions you have to make first thing, the less potential for stress. Get your clothes and bag ready the night before; decide what you are going to eat for breakfast.

3 Make sure your routine includes something to look forward to, every single day. To-do lists can dominate every waking moment, so use the model opposite to make sure you also schedule in time for those things that give you joy.

WHEN TO DO IT

These are habits to bring into every morning. They help set you up to notice the pleasurable moments of each day.

08 SWEET DREAMS

Sufficient sleep is absolutely key to happiness. Countless studies have found a direct correlation between a good night's sleep and a good mood. As little as one extra hour's sleep each night can make people feel a lot happier, and healthier too. Try the following tips for optimum sleep time.

1 Plan for at least seven hours sleep a night. Forty-two percent of Americans get less than this, but it's the minimum amount advised by the National Sleep Foundation. Work out what time you need to get up and work backward to see the time at which you need to go to bed.

2 During the day, make sure you get some natural light to help set your body clock—a half-hour walk at lunchtime is ideal.

3 An hour before bedtime, dim the lights and cut out all electronics, including phones and tablets. These emit "blue" light, which tricks the body into thinking it is daytime and blocks our production of the natural sleep-inducing hormone, melatonin.

4 Cognitive behavioral therapists believe it is important to set realistic sleep expectations. If you notice a tendency to exaggerate ("I can never sleep" or "I was awake all night"), be sure to answer back by forming a more helpful and truthful thought ("I'm not sure how I will sleep tonight, but I will see what happens").

WHEN TO DO IT

Every night. Try to get to bed at the same time each night, and get up at the same time each morning. A consistent routine will help you to form good sleeping habits.

DON'T WORRY!

Fears about getting to sleep stop you relaxing enough to do it. If you can't drop off, get up and do something calming, such as coloring or meditation. Go back to bed when you feel sleepy.

09 COLOR CREATIVE

Make time for some art in the morning. There's evidence to show that getting creative can make you feel happier. The concentration that is required for drawing, painting, or coloring puts your mind into a state that psychologist Mihaly Csikszentmihalyi calls "flow." Try this gorgeous coloring exercise; it is a great place to start.

WHEN TO DO IT

You can color at any time of day, but this is a great way of introducing a little creativity into your morning. Creating art can reduce anxiety while increasing feelings of self-esteem.

1 Gather together a few coloring utensils—you can use pencils or pens (if you are using pens, place a sheet of paper behind the design so the color doesn't bleed through the page).

2 Take a moment to sit and breathe. Remind yourself that you have these precious few minutes to enjoy yourself. You might like to set a timer, so you know you will have time to get ready for the rest of the day.

3 Look at your pencils or pens and pick up a color that appeals to you. Don't think too deeply about it, but go with your instincts. Start to shade a small area of the design, and let yourself enjoy the pure pleasure of coloring.

Turn the page: Try the coloring exercise overleaf.

SEE JOY IN THE WORLD

Even gloomy days contain moments of happiness, and most people have the opportunity to experience pleasure every day—if only we could allow ourselves to do so.

But many of us have what's called a "negativity bias"—we accentuate the negative and downplay the positive. This is one of the automatic negative thinking habits that we aim to address in cognitive behavioral therapy. By consciously taking note of the positives, we can train our minds to become more optimistic and open to joy.

You'll find some inspirational exercises to help you do just that in this chapter; others offer the mindfulness route. If you can live in the present moment, embracing your experience as it occurs, then you will be able to take greater note of the small everyday pleasures: the warmth of the sun, the first sip of a cup of coffee.

More than that, when we bring full awareness to what we are doing, the worry and stress can fall away, leaving us free to notice all that is right with the world around us. It is not just a useful tool, it is an attitude of mind, and one that can transform life for the better.

10 LOVE NATURE

In mindfulness we discover that one way to be happy is to come into the present and to be aware of our experience as it unfolds, moment by moment. Mindfulness requires concentration, and there are many ways to improve your focus. Try this beautiful little exercise. Not only will it enhance your observation skills, it will also help you to notice all the tiny cheering details that exist in your world.

1 Place a small natural object on a table before you. It could be a flower, a leaf, a shell, or a pine cone. Look at it, noticing its shape, its colors, the light and shaded areas, or any recurring pattern. Do this for a minute or two. If your attention drifts away, simply acknowledge this has happened and bring your focus back to the object.

2 Now pick up the object. Notice how it feels to touch—whether it is rough or smooth, soft or hard, its heaviness or lightness in your hand. Spend another minute examining every aspect of its feel, noticing those areas that feel different than others.

3 Bring the object to your nose and breathe in. Most natural objects have some sort of aroma— what do you notice about this one? Spend a further minute examining your object: smelling it, feeling it, looking at it, appreciating every aspect of it. Then put it down on the table again.

4 Gradually widen your focus out to your surroundings, taking in what you can see before you and in your peripheral vision. Slowly look around you, take note of what you can see. When you have finished, get up gently.

WHEN TO DO IT

This is an exercise that you can do occasionally or, alternatively, make it a focus exercise that is part of your daily routine.

11 SILVER LINING

Here is a visualization you can use if you find yourself depressed by tragic events that go on in the world. It's inspired by the often-quoted advice of Mr (Fred) Rogers, the children's TV personality, whose mother told him to "look for the helpers" whenever he saw scary events reported in the news.

1 Close your eyes and make yourself as relaxed and comfortable as you can; you can do this exercise sitting or lying down—whatever feels right.

2 Visualize the upsetting event as a dark and oppressive cloud in the sky. Try to paint a detailed picture of this cloud. See how the cloud billows out in some places and has patches that are very dark in color, while others are lighter.

3 Now imagine that you spot one patch of cloud that is significantly thinner and lighter. As you look at it, you realize that you can just discern the sun behind it. As you watch, there forms a tiny break in the cloud and a silvery light breaks through. You see this beautiful light and realize that a silvery light also shines in the dark cloud of human events.

WHEN TO DO IT

Do this as you need to. It's a good idea to limit your exposure to upsetting news, especially when you are winding down in the evening. Make a point of avoiding the more sensationalist stories and channels, too.

12   TURN OVER A NEW LEAF

Routines are useful because they provide the structure of our days. But they can also close our eyes to the wonder of everyday life. Being mindful means experiencing the freshness of every moment, which can increase our capacity for happiness. New experiences also help to jolt us out of complacency, and this strengthens our ability to be mindful. Try these three ways to disrupt your day creatively and turn off the autopilot.

WHEN TO DO IT

Break a habit or try something new each day to keep your mind alert.

1 What's your routine? Do you always walk the same way to work? Sit in the same chair when you watch TV? When we do things exactly the same way, it's harder to stay present. Do just one thing differently today and take the time to notice how your experience is different, moment by moment.

2 Do an everyday task with your non-dominant hand—clean your teeth, shave, eat. You'll realize how complex such operations are, and will stay mindful while doing them.

3 Look inside your wardrobe. Are there obvious themes? Buy a new item of clothing—one that you like, but that is unlike anything you already own, a color or a style that is new to you. Note how you feel the first time you put it on and go out in it.

PERSONAL AFFIRMATION

Every day
brings
new
discoveries

13 SOAK UP THE BEAUTY

We will all come into contact with pain, loss, or suffering at some point in our lives. In such times it takes effort and a true desire to be joyful. Repeated exposure to a positive stimulus is a cognitive behavioral therapy strategy to help us remember to think positively. If each day we do something that supports the fact that there is natural beauty in the world, we are more likely to look for that loveliness around us and feel more positive inside. Start and end each day soaking up the beauty in the world that surrounds you.

1 Listen for the sound of birds chirping as you walk about outside.

2 Take in the lovely smells emitting from the flower beds or bushes you pass.

3 Occasionally look up at the magnificent sky and watch the beautiful cloud formations.

4 Toward the end of the day, step outside and catch the sunset.

WHEN TO DO IT

Try this exercise three times a week for one month until it becomes more clear that living joyfully is possible—even in the face of difficulty. Gradually you'll be able to recover, rebuild, and find more joy in the world.

14 FOREST BATHING

Next time you are feeling low, go "forest bathing," the Japanese term for spending therapeutic time in woodland. Being surrounded by nature makes us feel happier and healthier, and seems to have particularly positive effects on our mental well-being. Forest bathing has proven to significantly increase vigor, and reduce feelings of anxiety and anger.

1 The point of this exercise is relaxation and spending time among trees. Aim to walk for 1.5 to 3 miles (2.5 to 5km) a day.

2 Once in the forest, revel in the experience of your senses. Notice the chirping of the birds or the crunch of branches underfoot. Feel trees as you pass them. Note the beautiful greens and browns of the natural world and the wonderful aroma of the forest.

3 Respond to the needs of your body. When you notice a feeling of weariness, find a spot that appeals to you, and spend time just sitting and enjoying the beauty of this natural place.

WHEN TO DO IT

Do this exercise when you can—once a week or once a month, depending on the accessibility of a forest.

PARK LIFE

Make time for a mini "forest bath" at least once a week by going for a stroll in a local park.

TOP **FIVE** WAYS
to increase your outdoor time

Have a daily walk with your partner,
friend, or dog

~~~~~~~~~~~~~~~~

Socialize outdoors: go for picnics,
hikes, cycle rides

~~~~~~~~~~~~~~~~

Do your exercise in nature
for a "green workout"

~~~~~~~~~~~~~~~~

Go sit in the park each day—read
a book, knit, or color

~~~~~~~~~~~~~~~~

Take a photo every day and document
the changing seasons

~~~~~~~~~~~~~~~~

15 A WARM WELCOME

What is more enjoyable than having a faithful companion greet you at the door? Unfortunately, not all of us can expect an effusive greeting every day. By using the cognitive behavioral therapy technique of cognitive reappraisal, however, we can encourage our brains to replace any negative expectations with positive thoughts. Try this visualization and rejoice in having your presence welcomed.

1 All of us have seen a dog go crazy when reunited with its owner. Try to imagine what it would be like to be greeted with the same excitement every time you opened a door.

2 The next time you are about to turn the latch on a door, envisage an imaginary loyal buddy waiting on the other side, eagerly wagging its tail.

3 Notice the flow of positive energy filling up your being as you pass through the door.

WHEN TO DO IT

Find the time to try this exercise at least three times a week, just before you open up a door. Over time, see how many more joyful and welcoming faces you notice throughout your day.

16   TUNE IN

You can lift your mood simply by listening to rousing music. A study at the University of Missouri found that people listening to upbeat music experienced an increase in the feel-good chemical dopamine, which affects two areas of the brain. The first area is connected with pleasure (the rear striatum) and the second with anticipation (the frontal striatum). Try this mindfulness-of-music experiment to see if you can replicate the results.

1 Start by choosing a happy track, either from your own collection, or by searching an online music-streaming service.

2 Listen to the music in a room in which there is minimal other noise, and put away obvious distractions (don't read or play on your phone while you are listening).

3 Take time to get comfortable and enjoy a few deep breaths before you put the track on. Remind yourself that you are listening to this in order to make yourself feel happier—setting your intention is an important part of the exercise.

WHEN TO DO IT

Do this every day for a couple of weeks, but vary the music from time to time. This exercise can be a wonderful addition to your morning or evening routine.

BE AWARE

This exercise only works if you make a conscious effort to listen to the music, and if you are aware that you are doing it specifically to improve your mood.

4 Once the music is playing, close your eyes and immerse yourself in the sound. From time to time, you may become distracted by thoughts or feelings. When you notice that you have lost focus, just gently bring your attention back to the music, no matter how many times this happens.

5 Be aware that music can be very evocative and can take your mind back to memories or trigger storytelling. Again, if you notice this happen, just bring your mind back to the music.

6 At the end of the composition or track, give yourself a few moments to stay where you are, eyes closed, breathing calmly.

7 Check in with how you feel, but don't worry if you don't notice any change in your mood. Becoming preoccupied with whether or not the exercise is working can be counterproductive.

MUSIC CHOICES

Choose a music genre that you enjoy, but make sure it has an upbeat tempo—something that cannot fail to boost your mood.

PERSONAL AFFIRMATION

Music
makes
me feel
happy

17 LOOK UP

If you work at a computer for hours at a time, then you may find your mood lowers as the day goes on. According to research at San Francisco State University, we find it easier to access negative thoughts and memories when we look down, and happy ones when we look up. Try these ways to remind yourself to look up from the page or the laptop screen.

1 Place inspiring messages and pleasing images somewhere above your eye line, but in sight of your seat at your desk. When you raise your head to see them, that physical act naturally brings your body into a more upright sitting posture.

2 As you walk to and from work, make a point of looking up at the sky from time to time. Whether the sky is gray or a sunny blue, its very immensity can give you an emotional lift.

3 Be sure to leave the office and go for a walk at lunchtime, to get a midday dose of the skies above. The exposure to natural light also helps your mood (see pages 16–17).

WHEN TO DO IT

Make looking up a frequent habit. If you work sitting down, stand up often to stretch your spine and change your visual perspective. Roll your head slowly up and down to take in the ceiling and floor.

18 FIND THE POSITIVE

Complaining can be a distorted and unhelpful way of thinking—it can also become a habit. In emotional brain training, we aim to replace this negative inclination with a positive one; our brains are flexible and can learn new ways of interpreting the information they receive through the senses. Try these two simple techniques to rewire your brain toward the positive things in life.

1 Stop what you are doing at regular intervals. Think of something good that has happened in the past hour. It can be something seemingly insignificant, such as that cup of tea you enjoyed, or something larger, such as the sense of clarity and purpose you are feeling. If you can't think of anything, stand up, relax your body, and take a deep breath in and out. Enjoy this tiny moment of repose and note it as something that feels good.

2 As you go into a room, look for three things that you like about it—a pretty picture, the natural woodgrain of a table, a brightly colored string of lights. You can do this in any room of your home or in a room that you have never entered before. It can also be a good exercise to do as you arrive at work.

WHEN TO DO IT

Looking for positives is an inspiring habit to get into, so do these exercises daily.

19 GAZE AT THE STARS

This beautiful meditation is a way of letting go of the mind's wish to impose order on everything we see. Appreciating the sheer size of the world gives us a sense of awe, which helps to widen our focus away from our own self-centered needs. This in turn increases feelings of happiness.

WHEN TO DO IT

Regularly. Watching the moon as it passes through its monthly cycle can also be a wonderful way to tune in to the natural rhythms of our planet. Or you can treat this as an occasional exercise to open your mind to your place in the world, and the world's place in the universe.

1 Take a blanket out on a clear night and spread it on a patch of ground. Lie on your back and allow yourself a few minutes to relax. Breathe deeply.

2 Keeping your gaze soft, look at the moon without blinking for as long as feels comfortable. Notice any tendency to spot shapes or patterns in the dark spots. Try to experience the moon as a fascinating object that you have never looked at closely before.

3 Gaze at a patch of star-filled sky without becoming sidetracked by any constellations. Be aware of the spaces between the stars as well as the stars themselves. Slowly broaden your gaze to take in as much of the sky as you can see. Experience the beauty and vastness of the universe for as long as feels right.

Try this: Color in the stellar mandala to recall your sense of wonder at the vastness of the night sky.

FIND INNER HAPPINESS

Happiness depends far more on what lies within us than our external circumstances. Research shows that people have a genetic baseline happiness level that is influenced by personality traits such as sociability, stability, and a propensity for hard work.

It is thanks to this characteristic that, within time, many people are able to overcome life trials, such as divorce and bereavement. The same applies to good fortune as well as bad. So, although you may long to win the lottery or own a bigger house, these things are unlikely to make you significantly happier in the long term.

The good news is that you can raise your baseline happiness level, and this chapter shows you how, using meditation, mindfulness, and techniques drawn from emotional brain training and cognitive behavioral therapy. These approaches show how our thoughts can have a huge effect on how we feel, and emphasize the need to adopt a gentle inner voice. They show us how to find a sense of space and perspective, so we can connect with our inner happiness whatever our situation.

20 SOUL FOOD

There are plenty of claims for "good mood" foods, but the link between diet and happiness goes beyond fads. We need good nutrition to stay physically healthy, but it also helps regulate our emotions and maintain good mental health—so what is good for the body is also good for the soul. Here are three key ways that what you eat can help how you feel.

1 Eat regularly. If you skip meals, your blood sugar drops and you may feel low or irritable. Try eating a smaller lunch and dinner plus a few well-spaced snacks to keep your mood steady.

2 Go Mediterranean. This diet is rich in fruits and vegetables, whole grains, nuts, and olive oil, but also includes small amounts of good-quality protein foods, such as fish, meat, eggs, and pulses. These are a good source of amino acids, which are needed by the brain to make serotonin and other chemicals that regulate our feelings and moods.

3 Stay hydrated. When we are thirsty, we think less clearly and so may lose our perspective more easily. Keep water to hand and give yourself "cues" so that you remember to drink regularly— whenever you sit down, for example.

WHEN TO DO IT

Every day. Watch your alcohol and caffeine intake too, as both can have a negative effect on mood.

21 JOYFUL SURROUNDINGS

Make a point of having uplifting cues and positive reminders in the space in which you live. Just as outdoor surroundings can impact on our mood, so too do those of our home environment. Follow this two-point plan to ensure your environment is full of joy.

1 Clear out any mood-drainers. Go into a room of your home and make a mental inventory of what you find there. Are there reminders of people you no longer see or have fallen out with, old ornaments you never look at, or piles of papers that depress you? Consider each area in the room in a systematic way, seeing what catches your eye and noticing any negative feelings that occur. Take out any negative items and store them out of sight.

2 Find room for mood-enhancers. Choose items that spark happiness in you, or remind you of strongly positive memories. Photographs of loved ones can strengthen your sense of self and your connections to others. It is also good to have tokens of your achievements or of places in which you felt good about yourself—holiday snaps and souvenirs, pictures of you doing yoga or running a marathon, for example.

WHEN TO DO IT

Do each room in your home systematically, and then revisit this exercise periodically, perhaps once a month or so to ensure that you are maintaining a positive environment.

22 CAT NAP

There is no doubt that our positivity is affected by how much rest we get. When we get more sleep we have more coping ability and are less reactive to negativity. Emotional brain training supports the theory that we are more likely to reach a state of bliss when our brains are at rest and not as stressed. Try this exercise to reinvigorate your body and your mind whenever you need a refresh.

1 After a nice meal, find a comfortable spot at home in which to curl up and take a rest.

2 As you close your eyes try to slow down your breathing to a gentle purr.

3 Now try to replicate the peaceful contentment of a cat taking a quiet noon nap.

4 After a few minutes open your eyes, give a nice stretch and notice how calm you feel inside.

5 Whenever you are feeling stressed or depleated in your day, take a moment to recall how you felt while doing the exercise. Recall the sense of contentment and restfulness and feel reinvigorated in body and mind.

WHEN TO DO IT

Practice this exercise at least twice a week. Taking the time to reset with a nap can help you feel more balanced and happy. Of course you will not always be able to take a cat nap when you are stressed. At such times, use your memory of the sense of relaxation you achieved following this exercise to provide a quick refresh.

23 TICKLE TIME

Do you remember being tickled with a feather as a child? A playful light touch can trigger laughter, even when we are feeling sour. The mere thought of being tickled can set off our happy sirens where we can't prevent the overflow of giggles. According to emotional brain training positive imagery and laughter are part of our personal joystick. Both help us to bounce back rapidly from stress without becoming overwhelmed.

1 Take a minute to remember the last time you told someone you were very ticklish. Next, get in touch with those sweet giggles you used to utter when you were just about to be tickled.

2 Try to visualize being tickled by a feather in all your most ticklish spots. Feel the laughter rising in your being and hold it there for just a few seconds.

3 Practice this visualization whenever you are feeling overwhelmed or bored. Discover how, over time, you are much more prone to feeling balanced while allowing your natural laughter to come to the surface.

WHEN TO DO IT

Try this visualization to break up the stress or monotony of your day and infuse some playful laughter into the moment.

24 TAME THE MONKEYS

We are easily distracted by the random thoughts that clamor for attention. Since many of our thoughts are negative or unproductive, this can make us stressed and unhappy. Mindfulness teachers use the term "monkey mind" to describe this mental commotion, and say that we can learn simply to watch our thoughts—the monkeys—rather than be carried away by them. Over time, this helps us to maintain a sense of stability, which increases our capacity for happiness.

1 Sitting comfortably, close your eyes and breathe naturally. When you feel ready, picture a group of monkeys playing in the trees of a forest. Create as much detail as you can—see how they jump from one branch to the other, shrieking and chattering.

2 Be aware that you are sitting quite calmly, as you watch the monkeys. You are not one of them, and you are not in the trees with them. They have no power over you, the detached observer. Keep breathing and slowly let the image fade.

3 Use this image as you go about your day. When you find yourself distracted by an unpleasant daydream or a thought, picture it as a monkey in the tree, and then gently allow it to fade from view.

WHEN TO DO IT

Do this exercise for five minutes daily. Ideally, do it in the morning, before you get caught up in the events of the day. Then use it whenever you need to.

25 THE OASIS WITHIN

A mental image of your "happy place" can be an oasis of joy that you are able to return to at any point in the day. Creative visualization is an effective way to manage stress and relax the body—our minds can respond to an evocative visualization in just the same way as a real-life experience. And the best thing is that you design your own oasis.

1 Take a few moments to settle yourself comfortably—you can do this sitting or lying down. Focus your mind by taking a few deep breaths. Make a point of relaxing your jaw and letting your shoulders drop.

2 Allow your breathing to slow down as your body becomes more relaxed. Now close your eyes.

3 Start to create an image of your happy place. It can be a place that you know well, somewhere you have never been, somewhere entirely made up, or a place that combines elements of different places. You may like your happy place to be a desert oasis, a tropical beach, a cool woodland glade, a spot by a mountain lake—or an indoor space—say, your grandmother's kitchen where you played when you were young.

4 As you picture this place, start to sketch in more detail. If, for example, you are visualizing a tranquil beach scene—imagine what color the water is, and whether it is still or gently rippled by the wind. Is the beach sandy or one with pebbles? Has it been warmed by the sun? Are there trees around, or any animals or birds? What can you see in the distance and up close?

WHEN TO DO IT

The more you practice a visualization, the easier it becomes to recall the image, so try doing this exercise for ten minutes every day for a week. It is a lovely exercise to do at night, to help you relax before going to bed.

5 Immerse yourself in this beautiful place, using all your other senses to help create the most evocative image possible. So, imagine what sounds you can hear, the texture of the ground beneath your feet, the cool breeze on your skin, or the saltwater as you dip your hand in it.

6 Enjoy being in your happy place—explore it, walk round it, breathe in the peace and happiness you feel there.

7 When you are ready to end the exercise, take a mental snapshot of your happy place and remind yourself that it is there any time you wish to return. Gently let the image fade away as you return your attention to your breathing. Then slowly open your eyes and bring your awareness back to your actual surroundings before getting up slowly and getting on with your day.

FAMILIARITY IS BEST

It can help to do the exercise in the same place each time you do it, and in the same position. The more often you do this, the more your mind will connect this place and position with feeling happy and relaxed—and you'll find it easier to reach that blissful state.

26 BREATHE DEEP

Breathing exercises are one of the quickest ways you can make yourself feel happier. Used in many different therapeutic approaches, they are known to reduce stress and increase feelings of vigor. Try this simple exercise.

1 Lie on your back, with your legs bent and your feet flat on the floor. Find a comfortable position; put a low cushion under your head if you prefer.

2 With your hands on your belly, breathe in deeply. Feel your belly push up against your hands. Breathe out, your hands lowering again.

3 Imagine a small ball of warm light in your belly. As you breathe in, it grows bigger, warming your chest; as you breathe out, it shrinks a little.

4 Next breath, imagine the ball of light growing to reach your throat and hips, then shrinking a little. Breathe again, and it grows more still, reaching your shoulders and ankles. Finally, it fills your whole body.

5 With each breath visualize this warm light softening and relaxing your body; as you breathe out allow yourself to let go.

WHEN TO DO IT

Once a day. This can be a nice exercise to do in the evening, as part of your wind-down before bed.

TOP **FIVE** WAYS
to build regular meditation practice

Start very small—literally
one minute a day

Build the time up gradually

Tag it to another habit, such as
brushing your teeth or drinking your
first cup of tea

Think "same place, same time" each day

Commit to regular practice,
but forgive slip-ups

27 THE ROAD AHEAD

We can quite easily talk ourselves into unhappiness, and justify our unhappiness with evidence that does not fit reality—cognitive behavioral therapists call this cognitive distortion. Try this visualization method to counteract a tendency for "fortune telling," whereby you make negative predictions about the future but treat them as though they were fact.

1 Notice when you anticipate what will happen in the future in a negative way: "I won't go to the party, I know it will be awful" and "There's no point my applying for that job, I will never get it."

2 Take a deep breath in and out. Tell yourself: "This is a guess. I cannot predict what lies on the road ahead." Close your eyes, and imagine yourself in a future life in which there is only misery—do this as vividly as you can. This is negative fortune telling.

3 Try asking yourself: "If I was happy and confident, would I think in this way?" Now close your eyes and visualize your life in the future again. This time, imagine that you see a joyous outcome, making this as vivid as you can. Enjoy predicting a positive result.

WHEN TO DO IT

Do this whenever negative predictions lead you to avoid doing something that could actually make you happier.

WRITE IT DOWN

Write your negative predictions in a notebook, and then do the very thing you would usually avoid. Make a note of whether your original prediction came true or not.

28 CHECK IN

"Checking in" is a key concept used in emotional brain training. It involves consciously and regularly stopping what you are doing to take stock of your feelings. Once you identify what is happening in your mind and body, you can take action to step out of stress and into a state of connection and joy.

1 At regular intervals during the day, stop what you are doing and focus on whatever is going on for you right now—what feeling, mood, or body sensations are most prominent? Download a mindfulness bell app to your phone to help you.

2 When you check in, you may be rushing for no apparent reason, or tensing your shoulders, or feeling angry, or happy and free. Whatever you observe, take this moment to pause and to take a few deep breaths in and out. This is an opportunity to allow your body to let go of unnecessary tension.

3 Is there something simple you can do to give yourself greater ease or joy? Stand and stretch, perhaps, or drink some water; go for a walk to clear your head. If so, do it. Over time, these tiny actions help you to learn to move out of stress and create a more solid foundation for the habit of happiness.

WHEN TO DO IT

On the hour, every hour during the day or at random intervals.

HAVE A CUE

You may like to have a "check in" cue rather than use a bell. Choose a piece of jewelry you always wear, such as a ring or bracelet. Every time you catch sight of this item during the day, use this as a reminder to check in with yourself.

29 TAKE FIVE

Positive psychology, which examines those characteristics that enable a person to thrive, has shown that gratitude is a key part of happiness, and it is easy to train your mind to be more thankful for the good things in life. So next time things are getting you down, try this inspiring exercise.

WHEN TO DO IT

This is a good exercise to do each day, perhaps before you go to sleep at night. People who practice gratitude regularly report having higher levels of positive emotions.

1 Take a moment to pause and breathe. Take hold of a thumb with the fingers of the opposite hand. As you breathe in, bring to mind one thing—large or small—that you are grateful for in your life. Say you might want to acknowledge the support of a good friend, the pleasure you took in a cup of coffee, or the fact that you are healthy. Say silently to yourself: "I am grateful for this"—and name the object of your gratitude.

2 Move on to your index finger. As you gently hold it, come up with another thing to be grateful for: your home, the weather, the vase of flowers on your table. Take each finger in turn: the middle finger, the ring finger, the pinky.

3 When you have completed your five reasons to be thankful, pause for a moment before going back to your day.

PERSONAL AFFIRMATION

I hold happiness in my hand

30 BRIGHT THOUGHTS

In cognitive behavioral therapy we find ways to cut through negative automatic thoughts (NATs), bringing a more wholesome way of thinking. One way we can do this is by asking questions that allow us to test the mindset behind our thoughts. We also need to mind our language so that we do not send stress-inducing messages to the brain. Try these techniques.

1 How do you respond when people ask you how you are? Lots of us use negative understatement such as "not so bad" or "can't complain." Even if giving a quick, polite response, say something positive, such as "I'm really good, how are you?".

2 When you notice a negative thought about yourself, such as "nobody likes me" or "I look terrible" try asking yourself: Is this really true? Is there a better way of looking at it? When I don't feel this way, do I have a different attitude?

3 Avoid making half-kidding, sarcastic comments or exaggerating the negatives. If you say that your relationships are car crashes, or complain that you are "absolutely sick with stress," you create a negative mindset and start to believe what you say.

WHEN TO DO IT

Adopt these habits regularly. Little by little they will boost your happiness potential.

31 PATHWAY TO PEACE

This is a reassuring visualization that you can do to release the emotions of the day, building the quality of acceptance—a key attribute of mindfulness. Vary the imaginary landscape to reflect the highs and lows of your experience, but always bring it to a close with a sunset.

1 Sit or lie in a quiet place. Close your eyes and take a few mindful breaths. Imagine yourself on a pathway, the sun rising behind you. You are not sure where the path leads, but you follow it. There are trees beside it and you enter a forest. The journey is arduous—you realize you are walking uphill.

2 Just as you start to feel out of breath, the path gets easier and the trees thin out. You find yourself walking down into a beautiful valley. The path goes up and down, and twists and turns—through woods here and meadowland there.

3 You reach a beautiful spot where you can rest under a tree. Looking back, you see that the landscape is beautiful; the hills and valleys that you toiled up and down give it character and beauty. You notice that the sun is starting to set. It's the end of the day. Allow yourself to rest and enjoy the view.

WHEN TO DO IT

Try doing this each evening before, or when you are in bed, to help you release the day and drift off into peaceful sleep.

YOUR AWARENESS

Perform this exercise with the understanding that it's the ups and downs of your day that give it character.

32 POWER PLAY

Play brings us joy. When you focus on work and responsibilities all the time, life can get too serious, leaving no room for pleasure. Play might seem an indulgence because it has no ostensible purpose, but it is actually a great way to relieve stress. It's also an effective way to relate to others, release creativity, and even make us more productive. Try this inspiring exercise based on returning to the age of nine, which—according to one UK survey—is the age at which we are at our happiest.

1 Take a seat, close your eyes. Allow your body to relax as you take a few deep breaths.

2 Bring to mind an image of yourself when you were nine years old. Try to picture what you are wearing, what your hair or your clothes look like. Think about what you are doing. Perhaps you remember yourself on a climbing frame, riding a bike, playing ball, or with a jumping rope. Allow yourself to inhabit the body of this carefree, relaxed you. Enjoy—re-enjoy—the activity as you recall this happy memory.

3 Let the image slowly fade away and open your eyes. Remind yourself that this fun, carefree person is you, and that you can access these happy feelings through the power of play.

4 Think how you can bring play into your adult life. Try playing with children you know, meeting up with friends to play frisbee or ball, offering to walk someone's dog if you haven't one of your own, or do something simple like jumping rope, juggling, or coloring in. Make time for play.

WHEN TO DO IT

Incorporate playtime into every day. Think about the day ahead—how could you bring a more playful attitude to work, to dinner time, to the quality time spent with your loved ones?

Turn the page: Try the coloring exercise overleaf to bring some play into your day.

SPREAD
THE JOY

Happiness and emotional warmth go hand in hand. Happy people are kinder to others and being kind to others is contagious—one good deed leads to another.

Kindness also raises the spirits of those who give. One study found that practicing loving-kindness meditation, in which you wish yourself and others well, made participants feel more joyful and, over time, strengthened their personal relationships. Not only that, but mindfulness and gratitude are also interlinked—when you are being mindful you start to appreciate the positives. By deliberately setting out to notice positives, you increase your overall awareness.

So making tiny incremental changes to your day—just by smiling at others on the street—can actually be a way of doing good in the world. And it helps you to feel part of a community, which is an important aspect of emotional well-being. So don't worry if it seems self-indulgent to tend your emotional health; in boosting your own happiness you will be spreading the joy to others.

33 THE DOMINO EFFECT

There is nothing more rewarding than spreading gratitude. We so often take the smallest things for granted and forget to say thanks. In our fast-paced lives, just noticing the kind things others do for us is not only reciprocal, but can multiply forward. Emotional brain training promotes the idea that our brain moves from a highly stressed to a joyful state when it receives key rewards, such as kind gestures. It is, however, up to us to pass those acts of kindness on to others.

1 Every time someone thanks you for something, consider passing some form of gratitude on to two more people.

2 Think of the different ways in which you can send gratitude. It could be in the form of saying thank you, writing a note of thanks, or just letting someone know how much they mean to you.

3 Once you have passed on your gratitude, reflect on how happy it made you feel, as well as those you thanked. Resolve to bring more gratitude into your everyday.

WHEN TO DO IT

Practice this exercise daily and see how actively expressing thanks can strengthen the bonds between you and others. It can bring a sense of inner calm and make us feel happy all at the same time.

34 TAKE A CHALLENGE

People who have social anxiety often deal with it by avoiding social situations . . . but that can make you feel isolated and unhappy. One of the tools in cognitive behavioral therapy is to challenge our fears by deliberately putting ourselves into situations that we find uncomfortable. Here's a simplified version of the technique to try at home.

1 One thing that holds us back from being more sociable is the thought of embarrassment or the belief that we won't be able to cope if others judge us. So start by considering how you think you would feel if you tried these "test yourself" challenges:
- Say hello to a stranger on public transport
- Ask a salesperson how his or her weekend was
- Go out with odd shoes or socks on
- Skip down a street
- Pay a compliment to a receptionist
- Sit in a colleague's preferred chair at a meeting

2 Now, grade your list from most intimidating to least intimidating. Pick the least intimidating and go out and do it. How did it feel? Was it different than you expected? If it felt uncomfortable, try doing it again tomorrow. If it felt fine, try doing the next thing on the list.

WHEN TO DO IT

Give yourself a mini social challenge every day for a week to help build your resilience. Use the challenges listed, or come up with some of your own.

35 LOVE THE WORLD

The loving-kindness meditation is an ancient practice that helps us to connect to our inner goodness, so that our positive loving feelings can flow freely. It's often taught alongside mindfulness, and there's evidence to show that practicing this beautiful exercise can boost feelings of contentment and joy as well as increase your empathy and compassion toward others.

1 Find a comfortable position, and spend a few moments breathing naturally and allowing your mind to settle.

2 Close your eyes and place your hand over your heart as you repeat these words in your mind, softly and gently: "May I be healthy and safe, may I be happy, may I live my life with ease."

3 Continue saying these words as you enjoy any warm feelings that you experience. Don't worry if you don't feel anything though, just keep your focus on saying the words.

4 Think of someone you love or like, and imagine that they are before you. Direct your words toward this person: "May you be healthy and safe, may you be happy, may you live your life with ease."

WHEN TO DO IT

Whenever you like. It can be a lovely exercise to do at the start of the day, or at the end of the day.

5 From time to time you will find yourself distracted—that's perfectly normal. When you notice this happening, gently direct your attention back to the words you are repeating.

6 Now think of an acquaintance for whom you have no strong feelings—the partner of a colleague, for example, or someone you pass on the way to work every day. Imagine this person is before you, and direct your words to him or her: "May you be healthy and safe, may you be happy, may you live your life with ease."

7 Think of someone you dislike, and, again, direct your words to him or her: "May you be healthy and safe, may you be happy, may you live your life with ease." This can be harder and it is best not to put yourself under pressure by choosing someone who invokes very strong feelings in you. Even so, you may notice negative feelings or thoughts that come up; as before, simply be aware of these and keep your focus on the words. Be gentle and don't judge yourself for any negativity.

8 Finally, direct these words outward, toward everyone in the world: "May we be healthy and safe, may we be happy, may we live our lives with ease." Continue for as long as feels right.

` WHEN TO DO IT

Loving-kindness traditionally starts with oneself, because it is easier to be kind and loving to others when we are compassionate toward ourselves. But if you are feeling bad about yourself, try starting with a loved one (Step 4) and then return to direct your kind wishes to yourself later on.

PERSONAL AFFIRMATION

May we live our lives with ease

TOP **FIVE** WAYS
to spread happiness

Say "hi" to your neighbors; offer help
to elderly folk who live nearby

Avoid gossip and give people the
benefit of the doubt instead
of judging them harshly

Make compassion a habit—do one
kind act a day

Listen well: Focus on hearing what
people say rather than offering solutions

Cultivate good manners: open doors,
say thanks, acknowledge others

36 . . . AND SMILE

Smiling has been shown to reduce frustration when we are under duress. The facial feedback hypothesis supports the cognitive behavioral notion that our gestures can influence our mood. The mere creasing of the corners of eyes and turning up the corners of our mouth can contribute to a positive shift in emotional state. This exercise helps you see not only how smiling can change your state of mind, but that of others as well.

1 Before leaving your home for an extended period, practice smiling in the mirror until it feels second nature.

2 As you leave your home and interface with the world around you, make a point, not only of making eye contact with everyone you pass, but smiling at them as well.

3 Notice how people naturally want to smile back at you. Also, observe how much better you feel inside.

WHEN TO DO IT

Practice this exercise every time you are out in the world. See how infectious your smiling is to those around you. Also, notice how smiling leaves you feeling more attentive and uplifted.

37 SPRING CLEANING

Try this exercise next time you have to face the dishes or some other household chore you dislike. It combines mindfulness with the concept of giving service, which is strongly linked to feelings of happiness. See if it works for you.

1 Before you start a chore, set your intention to do so with awareness and with love. Mentally note that your actions contribute to making your home a more pleasing place to be—for yourself and for the other people who live there.

2 Work without distraction and allow yourself to fully embrace the experience. If you are sweeping, note the heaviness of the broom in your hands, the subtle changes to the sound as you push and pull it. Or, if you are folding laundry, notice the feel of each item, the aroma of freshly washed sheets, the satisfying stack of neatly folded towels.

3 If your thoughts drift, gently bring them back to your experience in the here and now. Allow yourself to enjoy your chores rather than hurrying to get them over with.

WHEN TO DO IT

Always. If you have chores to do, it's much easier to accept that you are doing them rather than rail against them. In this way you are embracing the moment, rather than resisting it—a key tenet of mindfulness.

38 BE AWESOME

Try a little "awe therapy." Researchers from Stanford University have discovered that the awe we experience when viewing some breathtaking spectacle not only gives us an instant lift, it shifts our mental perspective and actually elongates our sense of time. As a result, we feel more patient and more compassionate—both of which help us feel happier.

1 Settle yourself into a comfortable position. Look at the picture of the Northern Lights. Now close your eyes, breathing naturally, and imagine yourself a little distance away from it, looking up at it.

2 As you visualize this incredible phenomenon, take the time to paint in as much detail as you can: the electric color of the air against the night sky, the dancing patterns created as the air swirls in the wind, the outline of the landscape bathed in its light. Try to experience the spectacle as if you were there, its glow illuminating your face.

3 Gently let the image fade before slowly opening your eyes and coming back to your immediate surroundings.

WHEN TO DO IT

This is a useful exercise for whenever you feel short of time and under pressure. If you find visualization difficult, try watching videos of natural phenomena—whales or waterfalls, for example.

39 RIPPLE EFFECT

If you want to be happy, be kind! Research shows that acts of kindness, whether small or large, precipitate a release of feel-good endorphins. More than that, when people are treated kindly, they become more likely to be kind to others. So one small act of kindness may set off a chain reaction of benevolence, like the ripples that emanate from a pebble dropped into a pool of water. Try these tips to get the kindness habit.

WHEN TO DO IT

Count your kindnesses every evening, before bed. It's a lovely way to end the day on a high note.

1 Count up the number of kind acts you have performed today. Simply noticing your own kind impulses can make you feel happier.

2 Find new ways to be kind. Let a car out in front of you, donate to a charity you believe in, pay for the coffee of the person behind you in the line, check in on an elderly relative or neighbor.

3 There is a huge amount of evidence to show that volunteering can also give you a burst of euphoria known as the "helper's high." This is also a great way to stay socially connected, which is itself an important part of happiness.

Try this: Color the pattern opposite and imagine each floral round as an act of kindness.

BUILD HAPPY RELATIONSHIPS

We are hardwired for intimacy. Countless studies show that people who have close relationships and a strong social network are happier and healthier than those who do not; they even live longer, too!

As with many aspects of happiness, there is a feedback loop of sorts: A good relationship leads to gladness, which in turn leads to better personal connections and deeper intimacy. This is because people who are happy tend to find it easier to maintain positive relationships.

By working on your own happiness, therefore, you are likely to strengthen your ties with your nearest and dearest. Not only that, but by using the exercises in this chapter to strengthen your relationships, you can up your overall happiness levels, too. It's a win-win situation.

Many of the exercises in this chapter can be carried out with a partner, but they work just as well with close friends or relatives. The key thing is to prioritize the person or people you care for most, and invest time and effort in making your relationships with them flourish.

40   STOP THE CLOCK

What would life be like if every time we spent quality minutes with those we loved, time stood absolutely still? According to emotional brain training, we need to be transparent and aware in order to achieve intimacy. By staying present, we slowly clear away our stress triggers and boost our capacity for loving companionship. Try this exercise to sharpen your awareness and improve your connectivity with others.

1 Imagine being frozen in time when you are with someone you care deeply about or love.

2 Take in the experience of being with this person, wherever you are. Pay attention to his or her features, gestures, tone of voice, and all the other things that make them uniquely special to you.

3 Try this numerous times until it becomes almost second nature, and watch your intimacy with those closest to you grow.

WHEN TO DO IT

Practice this exercise whenever you want to experience emotional connectivity with others. See how your ability to remain present grows along with your intimacy with others.

41 LET IT GO

Try this beautiful mindfulness-based exercise to help you experience forgiveness. Holding onto grudges is corrosive and can block us from feeling greater contentment in our lives. Those who can forgive the transgressions of others are happier than those who can't—and being forgiving generally can make you happier and healthier. Forgiveness doesn't mean reconciling with the person who has harmed you, if you don't want to; it simply means making peace with the past.

1 Sitting comfortably, bring to mind someone who has caused you pain in your life.

2 As you think of this person and the grudge you hold against them, notice what you are feeling. Do you feel angry or sad, irritated or nervous? Be aware of any physical sensations that occur in the body—a tightness in the chest, pressure in the throat, a twisting in the belly. Now attend to your thoughts—are they vengeful and unpleasant?

3 Acknowledge how this anger and resentment is affecting you. Ask yourself if you have carried the hurt for long enough? Are you ready to put it down? Are you able to forgive? Sometimes you might answer that question with a resounding "no," which is fine. Forgiveness comes in your own time.

4 If you feel ready, gently bring your attention to your breathing. As you breathe in, silently say to yourself: "As I breathe in, I acknowledge the pain." As you breathe out say "As I breathe out, I forgive."

5 Imagine you are holding a dandelion globe of seedheads, to represent your hurt. As you breathe out your forgiveness, your breath blows away one of the spores. Continue for as long as you like, or until all the spores have blown away.

WHEN TO DO IT

If you tend to bear grudges do this exercise regularly. You can do it at the end of the week, to let go of any small resentments that may have built up.

42 HELLO, GOOD-BYE

Intimacy is one of the key reward states that make us happy, according to emotional brain training. But when you have lived with someone for any length of time, it's easy to lose sight of the pleasure that you take in each other's company. Bringing conscious intent into your greetings and farewells is a good first step to bringing it back. Try this mindfulness-based transition ritual.

1 Rather than shouting a hello, go to your partner or other loved one as soon as you come into your home. Take a moment to make eye contact, and greet him or her affectionately. Likewise, when you leave your home for the day or any extended period, make contact and wish each other well.

2 During your hello/good-bye, try holding each other with full awareness for at least 20 seconds. A lengthy hug encourages the release of the "love hormone" oxytocin in the body, which lowers stress and promotes feelings of well-being and intimacy.

3 As you hug, bring all your attention to the feeling of holding and being held. Allow yourself to relax into the warmth and love contained in this embrace.

WHEN TO DO IT

Every day. A loving transition ritual should be a constant feature of your partnership, and of other loving relationships, too.

43 RIDE THE WAVE

Expressing every irritation or annoyance brings negativity into a relationship. Mindfulness teaches us that all feelings are temporary and pass in time, just as a wave reaches a peak and then dissipates. Try this visualization to manage your emotions without snapping at others.

1 When you notice feelings or anger or irritation, take some time out to sit quietly and be with the feeling. Often our reaction is to try and resist uncomfortable feelings, but this simply allows an emotion to follow its natural path.

2 Close your eyes and bring to mind the image of a glistening blue ocean. Imagine your feeling is a wave on the ocean of your mind. Watch as it gathers height and speed as it travels toward shore.

3 See the wave get higher and higher and then, as it reaches its peak, notice it crash over and then get smaller and smaller until it dissipates at the shoreline. Remain sitting and breathing calmly for a few moments before getting up slowly.

WHEN TO DO IT

Practice this visualization daily for a couple of weeks until it becomes very familiar to you and you can use it in stressful situations.

44 GIVE GENEROUSLY

There's a magic ratio when it comes to compliments and criticisms in a relationship—it takes five positive comments to balance one negative one. This correlation was established in a landmark study of couples and their likelihood of getting divorced. Use this fun visualization as a reminder to let the compliments flow freely and generously in your relationship.

1 Imagine your relationship as a collection box and each compliment you pay as coin in the slot, an investment in your happiness as a couple.

2 Make your compliments heartful and authentic. A powerful compliment is specific rather than general: "I love the way you look in that shirt," or "I really appreciate the way you bring me tea in the morning," rather than "You are wonderful."

3 Give a compliment at a time when the other person can hear it and not when he or she is rushing out the door.

WHEN TO DO IT

Every day. Giving compliments inclines the mind toward positivity because you need to be on the lookout for opportunities to give praise.

4 Make your compliments personal. Start with "I" rather than "You," so you express your feelings: "I was touched when you did ———"

5 Compliment a person's actions: By all means, tell your partner or friends they look great, but notice what they do, too, because actions go deeper than their looks.

6 When you give a compliment, be aware of any happy feelings this gives you. It can provide a temporary boost to the giver's own self-esteem as well as the receiver's.

7 Not everyone is good at taking compliments. If your partner or loved one shrugs off your comment, don't worry. He or she may still have received the positive boost that you intended, or it may kick in later. It helps to keep the focus on how he or she has made you feel. After all, you are giving a compliment because you want to, not in order to provoke a particular response.

ADD MORE!

Try doing a mental tally of the compliments you have given your partner or loved one in the evening—and add one or two more!

PERSONAL AFFIRMATION

Every day
I look for
ways to
express
my
appreciation

45 ANIMAL THERAPY

Animals help us to live in the moment and can be a source of great joy. Research shows that spending time with a pet can boost mood, relieve stress, and even lower blood pressure. Do this simple mindfulness-based exercise to enhance the loving bond between you and your pet. If you don't have a pet of your own, see if you can spend time with a friend's.

1 Every day, take the time to fully engage with your pet. Imagine this is your first encounter: Notice every aspect of his or her appearance, the shape of the body, each paw or claw, the face, the color and pattern of the fur or feathers.

2 Spend a few minutes petting your animal, noticing the warmth and other sensations you experience. Allow yourself to tune in to the sounds the animal makes as you immerse yourself in the sensory experience of connecting with it. Be aware of the heart beating beneath your fingers.

3 As you do this, think of the unconditional regard you receive from your pet, or the pleasure your animal gives you. Take a moment to allow appreciation for this animal's presence in your life to enter your heart.

WHEN TO DO IT

This is a good exercise to do each day. If you have a dog, bring mindfulness into your walks, too. Use this time to follow your dog's lead and enjoy the spontaneity and excitement with which your pet engages with the world.

46 LET THE SUN GO DOWN

Here are six dos and don'ts for happy relationships. They apply first and foremost to your relationship with your partner, but the same principles govern the way you should be with all your loved ones.

1 **Do** let the sun go down on a conflict. This is contrary to the popular saying not to let the sun set on a disagreement. In some cases, it may be best simply to acknowledge that there is an issue and set another time to resolve it. It is great if you can settle a difference easily, but upsetting conversations before bedtime can stop you sleeping, and this will likely affect your mood the next day. If possible, take a moment to honor the underlying connection between you before you sleep—saying goodnight, tell your partner that your connection is precious and more fundamental than any passing conflict.

2 **Do** be positive when you communicate. Try to bring a quality of mindful awareness to your speech: avoid exaggerations, criticism, and blame, and focus on expressing what you need. Attend to what the other person says too; often, we barely listen—so be present.

WHEN TO DO IT

Bear these principles in mind on a daily basis. Try looking at this list every week to check whether you are living by them.

3 **Do** the little things. Small acts of kindness, such as bringing your partner a cup of tea in bed in the morning or holding hands, help strengthen the bond between couples.

4 **Don't** stop trying new things. Doing novel and pleasurable activities together can increase feelings of intimacy. Try a new restaurant, go to a dance class together, explore a town neither of you know—or book a holiday somewhere completely different.

5 **Don't** block each other. Make it possible for each other to do the things that you want as individuals as well as a couple.

6 **Don't** neglect each other. Be prepared to put in some graft. All relationships need tending— think of your relationship like a garden that needs a bit of loving care in order to thrive.

KEEP LAUGHING

Laughter strengthens the bond you share. Seek out humorous films, go to comedy shows, and tell each other jokes.

TOP **FIVE** WAYS
to reconnect with a loved one

Write a list of reasons for
loving each other

~~~~~

Create ritual—share morning coffee or
set the table and dim the lights for dinner

~~~~~

Bury a time capsule with objects that
symbolize your relationship

~~~~~

Set digital boundaries—no phones
at the dinner table or in the bedroom

~~~~~

Cheer each other on. Support your
loved one's hopes and dreams

~~~~~

47 ENJOY THE JOURNEY

A flexible attitude is often considered key to navigating and maintaining balance in a relationship. Cognitive behavioral therapy emphasizes converting polarized thinking into more accepting patterns of thought for the purpose of strengthening bonds and managing personal conflicts. Try this exercise to help you treat personal differences as a learning journey.

1 Think of the last time you and your partner had a spat. You may have wanted to be heard, loved, and understood, but instead escalated the disagreement to the point of hurting each other.

2 Now try to imagine that same argument, but switch your thinking to how much care, respect, and love you have for that person.

3 Consider ways in which you could have been more open, playful, and less spiteful. Working with the same conflict, replay your responses using a more flexible approach, until you can chuckle to yourself when reflecting back on it.

4 The next time, you have a difference of opinion with someone you love, try to take an easier point of view and enjoy a less bumpy road.

WHEN TO DO IT

Consider doing this exercise after every disagreement you have with someone you love. By reshaping your responses, you can gradually see yourself responding more comically and flexibly when dealing with personal differences.

48 TREASURE MEMORIES

Make a point of sharing positive reminiscences with your loved ones. Reliving happy memories is a bonding experience, according to researchers at the University of North Carolina, and can benefit your relationship. You can also share in the glow of another person's experiences with this mindful-listening exercise.

1 Ask your partner, friend, or loved one to tell you about something good they experienced today.

2 As they talk, practice "active listening": make eye contact and attend fully to what he or she is saying.

3 React with positivity—by smiling and nodding, and by using affirmative phrases such as "how wonderful," or "that's interesting, tell me more."

4 Ask "open questions." These are questions that can't be answered "yes" or "no," so encourage the other person to elaborate: "How did you feel when that happened?"

5 At the end of the conversation, express your pleasure that he or she has shared this with you.

WHEN TO DO IT

This is a good exercise to do daily with a partner or family member; you can do it on an if-and-when basis with colleagues, friends, or acquaintances, too. Be sure to keep your focus on the other person's experience rather than jumping in with stories of your own.

49 FOSTER FRIENDSHIP

If you want to spread a little joy, foster positive friendships. There is increasing evidence of the importance of social connections in determining how happy you are, and even how healthy you are. And, of course, that works for both you and your friends. Here are three ways to prioritize friendship.

1 Have a "social hour" in your diary: An hour that you spend calling or emailing people that you want to see, to make arrangements or just to chat.

2 If your friends don't know each other, make a point of introducing them and of meeting their friends. It's easier to catch up with groups of friends rather than lots of individuals, because there are more people to do the suggesting and organizing.

3 Combine socializing with something you are interested in. Crafting circles and book clubs can be a great way of focusing a social event around a favorite hobby. Why not set up an adult craft circle, or similar, in a friendly local café?

WHEN TO DO IT

You may not manage a "social hour" every day, but be sure to put it in your weekly diary, and aim to see friends as often as you can. Friendship needs to be an integral part of your life, not an optional extra.

50 FIND THE RAINBOW

The intense emotions and excitement that feature at the start of a romantic relationship naturally settle over time. But it is important to keep a sense of spontaneity and joyfulness alive. Try this vibrant visualization to help you get in touch with the positivity of your partnership.

WHEN TO DO IT

This is an occasional meditation you can practice when you are feeling stuck in a routine. Come up with one positive surprise you can do for your partner or loved one—a small gift or a suggestion of an outing that he or she will like, say.

1 Sit comfortably and close your eyes. Spend a few moments breathing mindfully, noticing how you feel in this moment and allowing your body to relax little by little. Then bring into mind a sky that is filled with clouds and rain.

2 Imagine that a beautiful rainbow appears amid the clouds. Enjoy looking at the shimmering arc of color, then slowly bring the rainbow toward you in your mind's eye, so that you are engulfed in its color and light.

3 Do this for as long as feels right to you, and then gently allow the image of the rainbow to fade away. Allow yourself to return to the here and now and reflect on the beauty and color that is still present in your relationship with those you love.

Try this: Color these balloons in rainbow shades.

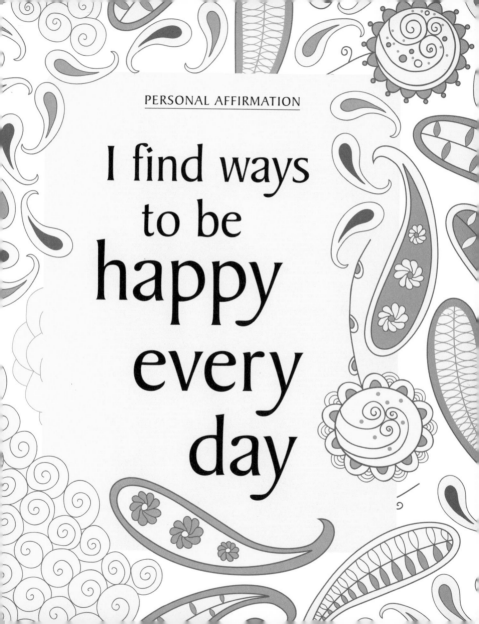

PERSONAL AFFIRMATION

I find ways to be happy every day

ACKNOWLEDGMENTS

Picture credits 2–3 (and side detail throughout book) Oksancia/Shutterstock 6 ittipon Munmoh/ Shutterstock 9 CHOATphotographer/Shutterstock 11 niki_spasov/Shutterstock 12–13 mcherevan/ Shutterstock 15 Oksana Shufrych/Shutterstock 16 Vaclav Volrab/Shutterstock 18 Julia Sudnitskaya/ Shutterstock 20–21 Nila Newsom/Shutterstock 22 Antonova Anna/Shutterstock 25 Byjeng/ Shutterstock 26 Suzanne Tucker/Shutterstock 28 mcherevan/Shutterstock 30 Sherrod Photography/ Shutterstock 32 Baleika Tamara/Shutterstock 34 Anna Levan/Shutterstock 37 Nattapol Sritongcom/ Shutterstock 38–39 il67/Shutterstock 40–41 antalogiya/Shutterstock 43 Business stock/Shutterstock 44 Repina Valeriya/Shutterstock 46 Passakorn sakulphan/Shutterstock 49 antalogiya/Shutterstock 50 Bachkova Natalia/Shutterstock 52 Subbotina Anna/Shutterstock 54–55 Suzanne Tucker/Shutterstock 56 Halfpoint/Shutterstock 58 BrAt82/Shutterstock 60 antalogiya/Shutterstock 62 Dariush M/ Shutterstock 64 tomertu/Shutterstock 67 Snezh/Shutterstock 68–69 Maria_Galybina/Shutterstock 71 THPStock/Shutterstock 72 roberto scaroni/Shutterstock 74 aquatti/Shutterstock 76 Dalibor Valek/ Shutterstock 78 Liliya Linnik/Shutterstock 80 tratong/Shutterstock 82 Victor Lauer/Shutterstock 85 Tortoon Thodsapol/Shutterstock 86 ampcool/Shutterstock 88–89 Konstanttin/Shutterstock 90 Tupungato/Shutterstock 92 BrAt82/Shutterstock 95 Maria_Galybina/Shutterstock 96 TZIDO SUN/ Shutterstock 98 Creative Travel Projects/Shutterstock 100 Annette Shaff/Shutterstock 102–103 OlichO/Shutterstock 104–105 antalogiya/Shutterstock 107 PongMoji/Shutterstock 108 natalia bulatova/Shutterstock 110 aimy27feb/Shutterstock 112 takasu/Shutterstock 115 antalogiya/ Shutterstock 116–117 hofhauser/Shutterstock 118 Pavinee Chareonpanich/Shutterstock 120 Vasilyev Alexandr/Shutterstock 122 Jamen Percy/Shutterstock 124 sliplee/Shutterstock 126–127 Maria_ Galybina/Shutterstock 129 zixian/Shutterstock 130 Mckyartstudio/Shutterstock 132 Daniel Gale/ Shutterstock 134 MorganStudio/Shutterstock 136 Geoff Hardy/Shutterstock 138 Melpomene/ Shutterstock 141 Maria_Galybina/Shutterstock 142 Annette Shaff/Shutterstock 144 Kletr/ Shutterstock 147 iravgustin/Shutterstock 148–149 Photo Boutique/Shutterstock 150 Dudarev Mikhail/Shutterstock 152 Sunny studio/Shutterstock 154 MJ Prototype/Shutterstock 157 Lolla Lenn/ Shutterstock 158–159 Lisla/Shutterstock

Cover: Oksancia/Shutterstock

While every effort has been made to credit contributors, Quantum would like to apologize should there have been any omissions or errors, and would be pleased to make the appropriate corrections to future editions of the book.